i spy with my littl[e eye] something beginning with...

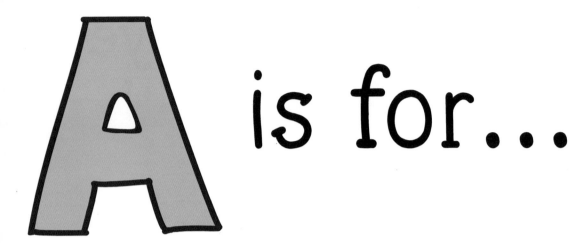 A is for...

ALLIGATOR

i spy with my little eye, something beginning with...

B is for...

Bee!

i spy with my little eye, something beginning with...

C

Chicken

i spy with my little eye, something beginning with...

D+E

D is for...

Dog!

E is for...

Elephant!

i spy with my little eye, something beginning with...

F is for...

Fox!

i spy with my little eye, something beginning with...

G is for...

Goat!

i spy with my little eye, something beginning with...

H is for...

Horse!

i spy with my little eye, something beginning with...

i is for...

Iguana!

J is for...

Jellyfish!

i spy with my little eye, something beginning with...

K is for...

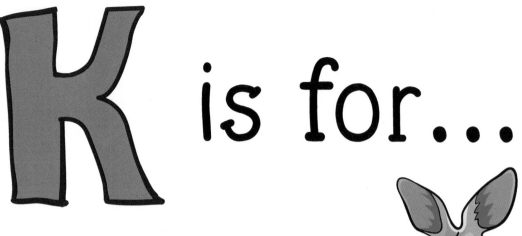

Kangaroo!

i spy with my little eye, something beginning with...

L is for...

Lion!

i spy with my little eye, something beginning with...

M is for... Monkey!

N is for... NARWHAL

i spy with my little eye, something beginning with...

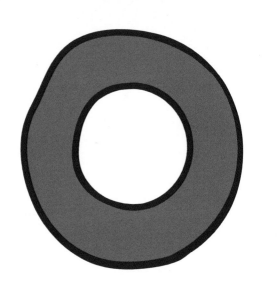 is for...

Octopus!

i spy with my little eye, something beginning with...

P is for...

Panda!

i spy with my little eye, something beginning with...

Q+R

Q is for... Quail!

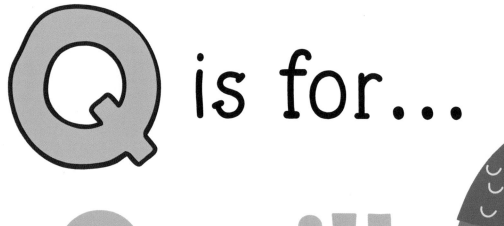

R is for... Rat!

i spy with my little eye, something beginning with...

S is for...

Spider!

i spy with my little eye, something beginning with...

T + U

T is for...
Turtle!

U is for...
Unicorn!

i spy with my little eye, something beginning with...

V is for...

Vulture!

i spy with my little eye, something beginning with...

W+X

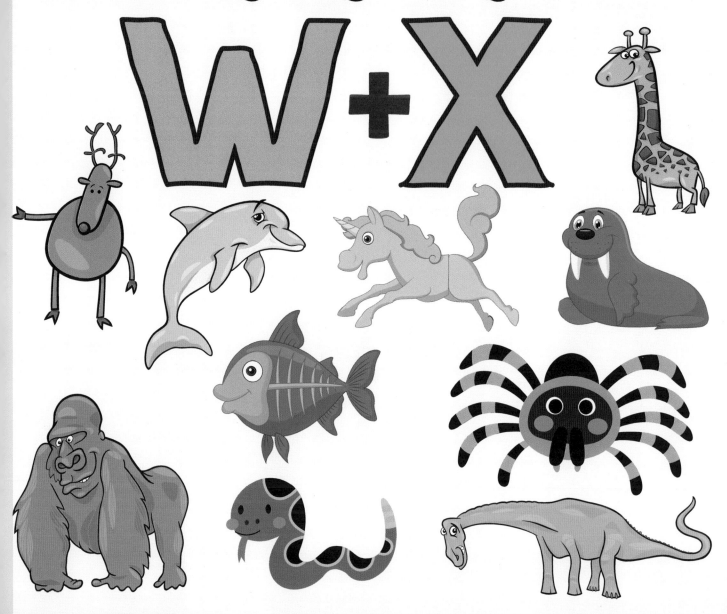

W is for...

Walrus!

X is for...

X-ray fish!

i spy with my little eye, something beginning with...

Y+Z

Y is for...

Yak!

Z is for...

Zebra!

Printed in Poland
by Amazon Fulfillment
Poland Sp. z o.o., Wrocław

59283216R00026